MICAH

Kenzie
Lull :)

MICAH

THE MIGHTY MARATHONER
& HIS FRIENDS

Mackenzie Snell

pictures by
Nathan Shields

BeaLu
BOOKS

*To Evan, and all the other amazing friends out there,
and to anybody who might need a friend.*

This is Micah and he loves to go to school.

School is a little different for Micah because of how his brain was made. Our brains are made up of two different sides. One side of Micah's brain doesn't talk well to the other side. It makes moving, speaking, and playing hard.

Because Micah's legs don't work the same way as most kids, he uses a wheelchair to move.

Micah rides the bus just like everyone else. His bus is super cool. It has an elevator that helps him get on and ride to school.

When Micah gets to school, a lot of his friends are waiting. One of them is Micah's best friend, Evan.

Micah has two classes, two teachers, and a lot of friends at school.

Micah loves being with his friends. Anyone can be a good friend, and everyone needs a good friend.

Micah's friends are helpful, patient, and kind.

Micah and Evan love to laugh and play. Being a friend means helping each other. Evan loves pushing Micah around in his wheelchair.

Helping each other is fun. Micah likes to listen to Evan tell him about all of his adventures.

When Micah's friends need someone to talk to, Micah always listens to them and makes them happy.

Learning can be hard sometimes. Friends can help make it easier and fun! Sometimes it takes Micah longer, but Evan and his other friends are always patient.

Micah is patient with his friends too! He loves to listen to Evan read and sound out new words.

Micah communicates in a special way. It's hard for him to use words to talk. He uses different tools to talk with his teachers and friends.

Evan thinks the tools Micah uses to talk are awesome. He listens closely to Micah when they talk. Micah's friends have to be patient because sometimes it takes Micah a while to communicate.

Even though Micah can't talk the same way as others,
he still loves it when his friends are kind and talk to him.

Micah and his friends love to learn together. They like playing math games, reading, and singing and dancing.

Good friends are kind to each other. They take turns and share things. Micah always shares his ice cream with Evan.

Micah and Evan are best friends. They are helpful, patient, and kind to each other. Having friends is super fun!

Learn More About Micah and Micah's Miles

The Snell family's journey with Micah didn't go according to plan. He made his entrance into this world seven and a half weeks early and stayed in the NICU for thirty-eight days. Life began to blur with the doctors, specialists, medicines, and diagnosis. Micah's mom, Suzie, became the expert on sharing Micah's medical history in three to five minutes, over and over again. They learned about seizures and seizure medications. They learned about feeding tubes. Really, they just learned to survive.

The world constantly told them what Micah couldn't do, and it seemed like the only thing the Snells could do was just listen. Without the support of family and friends, they are not sure where they'd be. After a while, life started to settle into a new routine. They met other families who had similar experiences; they met organizations like the United Cerebral Palsy Foundation. Most importantly, they didn't feel as alone. The Snells were ready to start pushing back on the constant message of what Micah couldn't do because Micah is an amazing kid that can do so much.

Micah had always loved to be outside riding in a stroller, and the Snells really liked taking him on walks and for runs. Micah's dad, Jeff, was training for a marathon and they thought; why not take Micah? As they planned for the marathon, they started thinking about how they could use the experience they had to raise awareness and funds for some of the organizations that supported Micah. With that first marathon, Micah's Miles was born with the mission of building a community around Micah and inspiring others through his amazing spirit.

For each marathon, Micah partners with a cause that makes a difference for others. At ten years old, Micah had finished 33 marathons and raised over $70,000 for the partner organizations. Micah has the spirit of a runner; he understands perseverance and patience. It's really all he knows. That runner's spirit is a little light that shines out from him.

The Snells have the amazing opportunity to share Micah with the world. Micah's Miles brings people together and reminds them constantly of what a gift life is. They are very fortunate to have a Micah's Miles Team which consists of friends, family, and community leaders who have come together to help us all share Micah's story. Micah's sister, Mackenzie, and brother, Stephen, are a big part of Micah's life as well as grandparents and extended family. Micah loves school, and all his teachers and friends. He loves watching the Seattle Seahawks and Gonzaga Bulldogs and all his siblings' activities. He's also a huge fan of music and musicals.

This book is a glimpse into Micah, the importance of friendship and community through the eyes of his sister. The Snell family hopes it brings you joy and inspires you to share your light with others.

Micah, Mackenzie, and Suzie use this book in assemblies they present at schools. Micah uses a communication device to help with the lesson. They teach about friendship by reading the story and sharing how Micah and Evan are helpful, patient, and kind to each other. We hope you and your students enjoy reading *Micah the Mighty Marathoner and His Friends* and the lesson on friendship.

Micah the Mighty Marathoner and His Friends
Helpful, Patient, and Kind

Learning Target for reading and lesson:
Students will be able to state what being helpful, patient and kind looks like, sounds like, and feels like. Students will be able to complete the challenge of finding one, or more, people to be helpful, patient, or kind to in the next day or week. Students will feel the positive effects of being helpful, patient, and kind and will continue this challenge daily, finding one more people they can help.

Before reading:
Show students the cover of Micah the Mighty Marathoner and His Friends and ask:
- What inferences can you make?
- What predictions can you make?
- What do you know about being a friend?
- Who is Micah?

While reading:
Show students the pictures as you read. Stop and answer any questions the students may have as you are reading.

After reading:
Use these questions to guide your students in a classroom conversation, or circle discussion, about Micah the Mighty Marathoner and friendship:
- Turn and tell your neighbor your favorite part of the book and why?
- Turn and tell your other neighbor ONE idea you took away, or learned, from this book?
- Share with the group what you think Micah's friends have in common? (they are helpful, patient, kind)

- Think to yourself: Are being helpful, patient, and kind good qualities in a friend?
- Why?
- Now turn and tell your neighbor why you think this way?
- *Helpful:*
  - Why is it important to help others?
  - In our story, how did Micah help his friends?
  - What did it *look* like when Micah helped his friends?
- *Patient:*
  - Having patients feels different all the time, in our story how were Micah's friends patient with him?
  - Why do you think they were patient with Micah?
  - Think of the last time you were patient with a friend or classmate how did it *sound*? What words were you using and why?
- *Kind:*
  - In our story, Micah shared his ice cream with Evan, why do you think he did that?
  - It made Evan and Micah *feel* good inside to share and be kind to each other

Closing:
Now you know what being helpful, patient, and kind looks like, sounds like, and feels like; we think you are ready for a challenge! Go out and find at least one person to be helpful, patient, or kind towards each day this week and think about how it fills you up inside with good feelings. Keep that feeling ALIVE by continuing to be a good friend by being helpful, patient, and kind to as many friends as you can.

About the Author

Mackenzie Snell, Micah's sister, recently graduated from Camas High School in Camas, Washington, and will soon be attending the University of Washington pursuing a career in the medical field. Mackenzie also has a twin brother, Stephen, and a chocolate lab, Clara, and she loves to go on walks and spend time with both of them. She loves helping children with disabilities which is one reason she thinks she is so fortunate to have a brother like Micah.

About the Illustrator

Nathan Shields enjoys making art with his children and students. He lives in Port Angeles, Washington.

Proceeds from the sale of this book will go to Micah's Miles partner charities. Visit MicahsMiles.org for more information.

ISBN: 9781735364186

Library of Congress Control Number: 2020945906

Edited by: Luana K. Mitten
Book cover and interior design by Tara Raymo • creativelytara.com

Printed in the United States of America
September 2020

BeaLu Books
Tampa, Florida

www.BeaLuBooks.com

CPSIA information can be obtained
at www.ICGtesting.com
Printed in the USA
BVHW020525031120
592181BV00002B/3